Name _____

Earth - The Water Planet

Why is Earth called the water planet? Water is in the oceans (o-shunz). Water is on the land in rivers and lakes. Water is in the clouds (klowds) over the earth. We can find water almost everywhere on our planet.

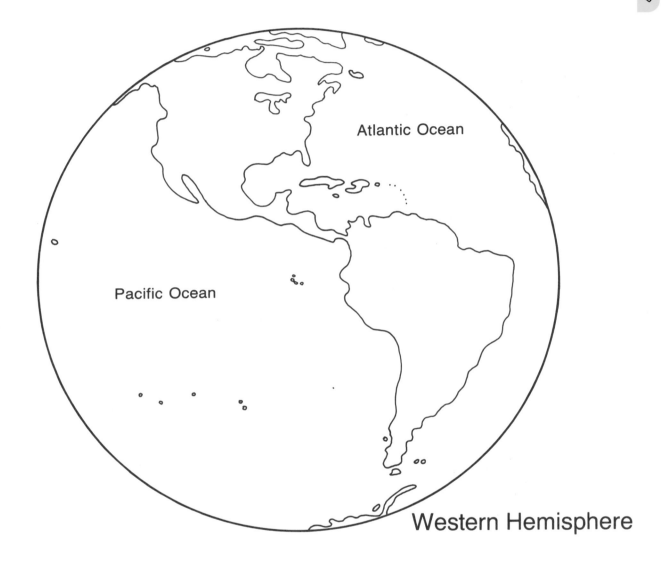

Atlantic Ocean

Pacific Ocean

Western Hemisphere

Color the oceans blue.
Color the land green.

Extra: On the back of this paper draw a place you can find water.

1

WATER

Name_____

Why Is Water Important?

Plants, animals, and people all need water to live. Plants use water to grow and to make food. Animals and people drink water to grow and to be healthy.

Plants and animals need different amounts of water.

X things that need a lot of water.
☐ things that need a little water.

People need water every day. We cannot live very long without water.

Extra: Have you had any water to drink today?

Name _____

The Water Cycle

The hot sun makes water change into water vapor. The water vapor goes up into the sky and makes clouds. Wind blows the clouds over the land. The clouds meet cool air. The water vapor changes back into water drops and falls to the earth as rain.

Color the water blue:

Extra: Draw a rain picture on the back of this page.

Teacher: You may want to introduce the term evaporation.

Name_____

Water In The Air

The hot sun warms the earth. The heat changes water to water vapor. Warm air is lighter than cold air. It goes up into the sky. The water vapor goes up with the warm air.

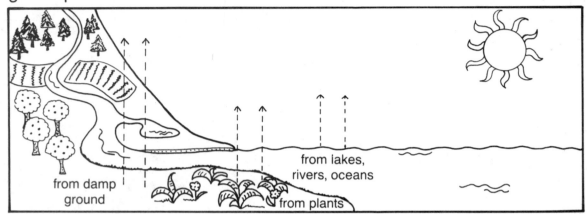

from damp ground

from lakes, rivers, oceans

from plants

Water vapor is always in the air, but it is invisible. You can see water vapor when you breathe out on a cold day. It looks like a little cloud when you breathe.

warm day   cold day

Yes or No

1. Warm air goes up into the sky.

2. You breathe out water vapor.

3. Heat changes water to water vapor.

Extra: Can you think of another place you can see water vapor?

Name_____

Clouds

Clouds can have different numbers of water drops in them. White, thin clouds have a little water. Dark, heavy clouds have a lot of water. Fog is a thin cloud of little water drops that comes to the ground.

Here are some clouds.

X the cloud that has the most water.

Sometimes clouds look like an animal or a person. Make a cloud picture on the back of this paper.

Extra: Look out a window. Circle the cloud on this page that looks the most like the clouds you see.

Name_____

Making a Cloud

When <u>warm</u>, damp air meets <u>cold</u> air, the water vapor turns into little <u>drops</u> of water. When millions of the little drops come together they make a cloud.

Fill in the blanks:

1. A cloud is made up of millions of [_____]

2. Water vapor turns into drops of water when [_____] air

meets [_____] air.

You can see water vapor turn into water drops:

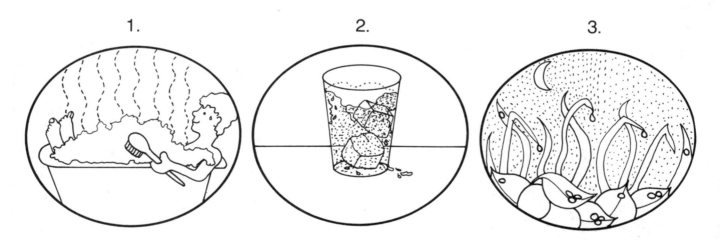

1.	2.	3.
When you take a hot bath and the warm air meets the cold mirror.	When you put cold ice cubes in a dry glass and the warm air meets the cold glass.	When the cool night air meets the warm ground. The water drops on the grass are called dew.

Extra: Color the pictures.

Name_____

Rain

Rain comes from clouds. When the little water drops get together, they make bigger drops. When the drops get too big and too heavy, they fall down to the earth as rain.

Draw you walking in the rain.

Don't forget an umbrella!

Extra: Add puddles and lightning to the picture.

Name _____

Rainbows

Sunlight is made up of many colors. We do not see the colors most of the time. When sunlight meets raindrops, the sunlight breaks up into its different colors. When this happens, we see a rainbow in the sky.

Color the rainbow.

red
orange
yellow
green
blue
violet

Sometimes you can see rainbows in different places.

What colors do you see in a rainbow?

8

WATER

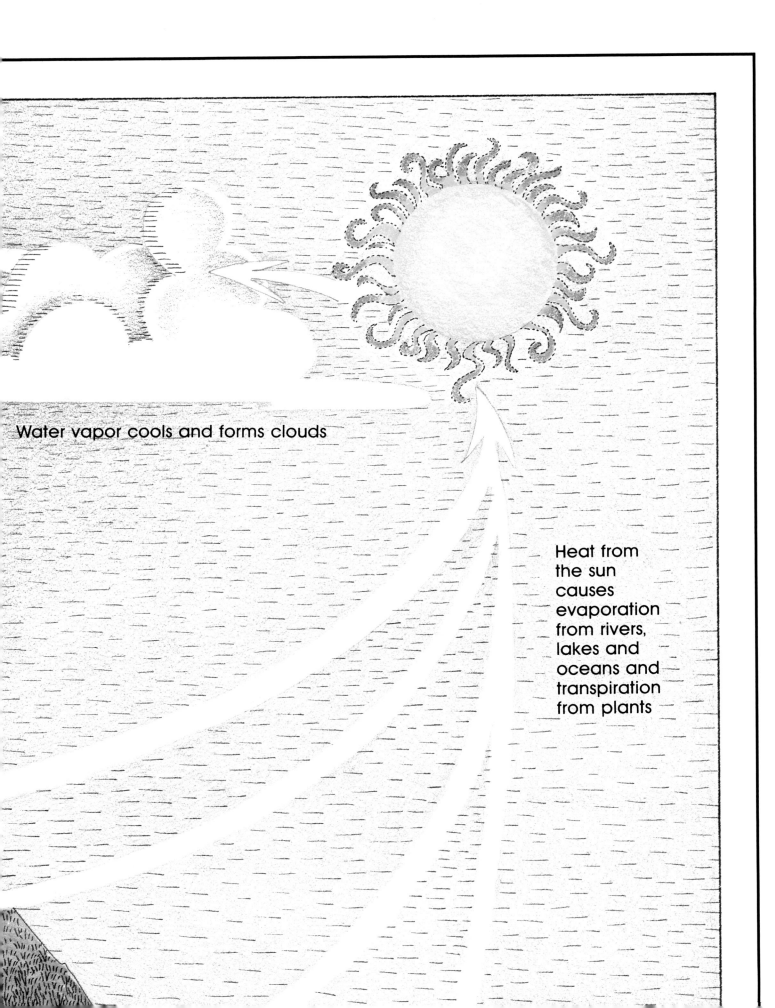

Water vapor cools and forms clouds

Heat from the sun causes evaporation from rivers, lakes and oceans and transpiration from plants

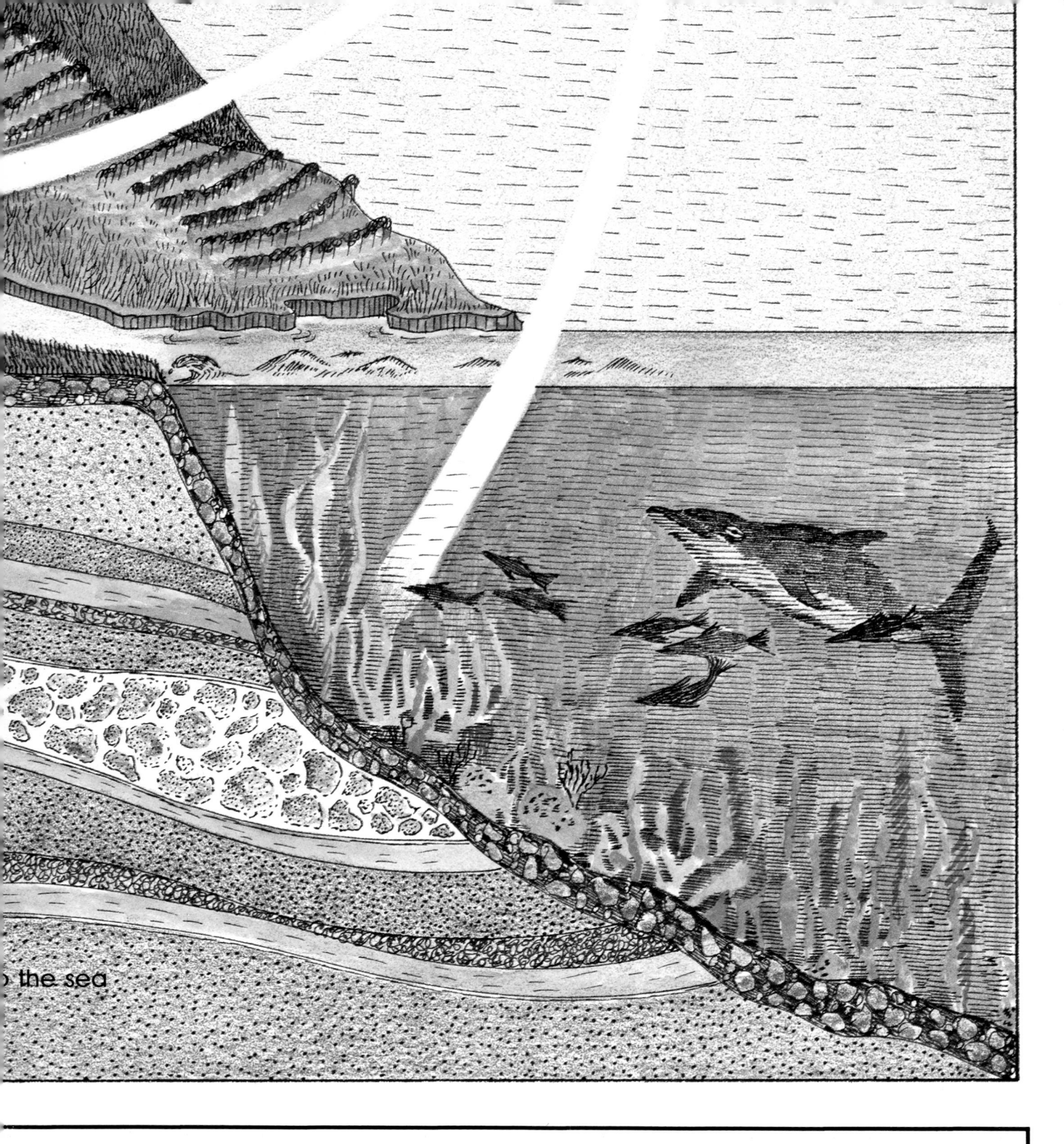

the sea

Cycle

Water

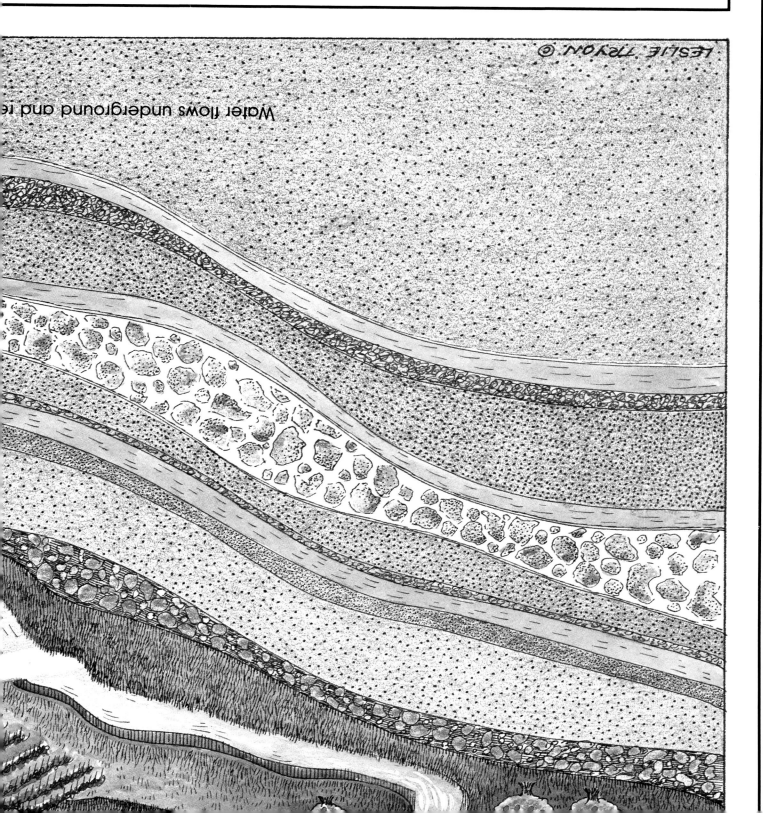

LESLIE TRYON ©

Water flows underground and re

Clouds cool
making rain & sno

Frozen Water

If it is <u>very</u> cold, the water vapor turns into frozen flakes of snow. The snowflakes fall to the earth.

All snowflakes have six sides, but no two look just alike. It takes millions of snowflakes to make one snowman.

How to make a snowflake:

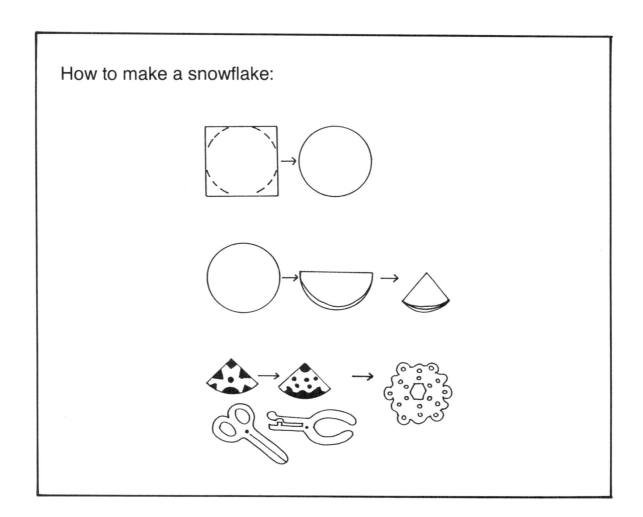

Sometimes on cold, windy days, balls of ice fall from the clouds. These balls are called <u>hailstones</u>.

Extra: Draw two different things you need in snowy weather on the back of this paper.

Make A Water Cycle Wheel

A.

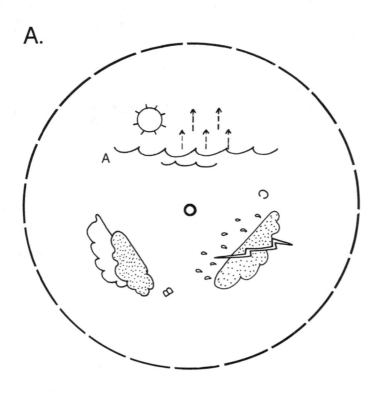

1. Cut out Part A and Part B.
2. Cut on the - - - on Part B to make a window.
3. Fold Part B.

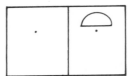

4. Put Part A into Part B and fasten with a 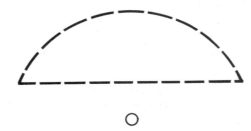.

front   back

5. Turn the wheel.

B.

fold

A. The water vapor goes up into the sky.

B. The water vapor becomes drops. The drops become clouds.

C. The water falls back to the earth as raindrops.

WATER

Name _____

Did You Know?

When water is liquid, we can drink it, wash with it, or swim in it.

Water can be a <u>solid</u> (so-lid). When water freezes into ice or snowflakes, it is a solid.

Water can be a <u>gas</u>. When water is warmed, it goes into the air as a gas.

| solid   liquid   gas |

Extra: Is soup a solid or a liquid?

WATER

How We Use Water At Home

X the places you find water at your house:

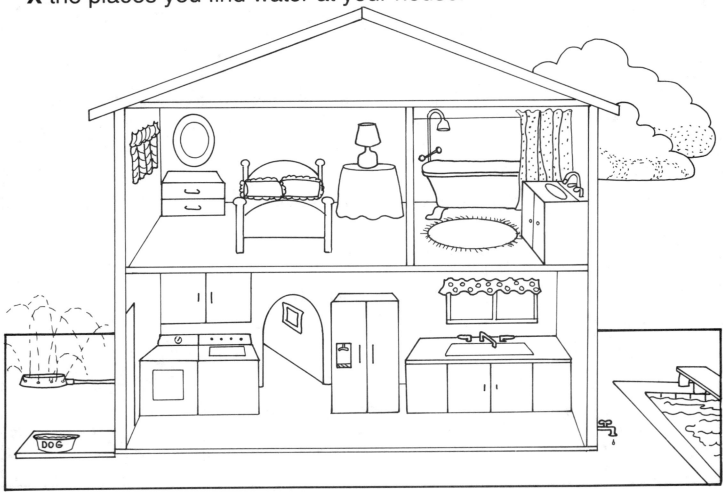

List 4 ways you have used water today.

1. _____
2. _____
3. _____
4. _____

Extra: Turn this paper over.
Show how you can use water for fun.

Name _____

How can water help make electricity?

Water can even be used to help make electricity (e-lek-tris-i-tee). Fast–moving water from a dam or waterfall turns a machine called a turbine (tur-bine). When the turbine turns, it spins magnets (mag-nets). This makes electricity in wire coils that are around the magnets. The electricity is carried away in cables (ka-bls).

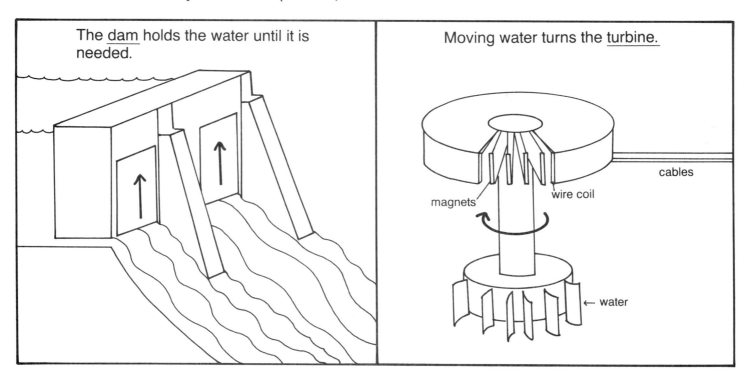

The dam holds the water until it is needed.

Moving water turns the turbine.

cables

wire coil

magnets

← water

Fill in the blanks:

1. Moving water turns a `_____`.

2. Electricity is carried away in `_____`.

3. `_____` are around the magnets.

4. Moving water can help to make `_____`.

wire coils
cables
water
turbine
electricity

Extra: Draw three ways you use electricity in your house.

1. Water that falls from the sky is _____ .

2. Flakes of frozen water that fall from the sky are _____ .

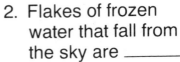

3. A curve of bright colors you see after the rain is a _____ .

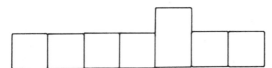

4. A block of frozen water is an _____ .

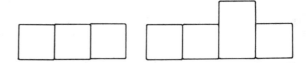

5. The fluffy white shapes up in the sky that can turn into rain are _____ .

6. When water boils it turns into _____ .

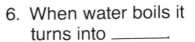
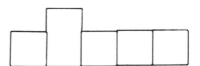

clouds   rain   snowflakes

ice cube   rainbow   steam

Extra: Put an X on the thing that is made when light hits water drops.

Name _____

Do You Remember?

A. List the words that tell about water.

1.
2.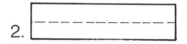
3.
4.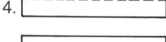
5.

6.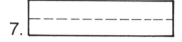
7.
8.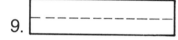
9.
10.

ice	wind	sun	snow
sand	steam	cloud	rock
fog	frost	water	rain
dew	hail	grass	glass

B. Can you find these water words?

___ cloud   ___ puddle
___ dew   ___ rain
___ frost   ___ river
___ lake   ___ snow
___ ocean   ___ steam
___ pond   ___ water

```
S T E A M R A I N
F C L O U D O P R
R T S L M E N U I
O C E A N W S D V
S R C K P O N D E
T B X E V Z O L R
W W A T E R W E N
```

Extra: Turn this paper over. Make a picture to show 3 kinds of water.

WATER

This is a variation of Bingo. Run a copy for each child. S_____ -9 to any box they choose. You may want to make the sunny "Weather Watch Winner" ba_____

Weather Watch

☁ 1	☁ 2	☁ 3	☁ 4	☁ 5	☁ 6	☁ 7	☁ 8	☁ 9
❄ 1	❄ 2	❄ 3	❄ 4	❄ 5	❄ 6	❄ 7	❄ 8	❄ 9
☀ 1	☀ 2	☀ 3	☀ 4	☀ 5	☀ 6	☀ 7	☀ 8	☀ 9
☂ 1	☂ 2	☂ 3	☂ 4	☂ 5	☂ 6	☂ 7	☂ 8	☂ 9

Run one copy per player.

Weather Watch!

☁	❄❄	☀	☂

Use beans, paper squares, buttons, or whatever else you feel is appropriate for your students to cover the numbers as they are called.
"Cloud 6. Sun 4. Etc.. . . ."

EVAN-MOOR CORP., 1986

16

WATER